I0453578

"Out of the dark hole of grief comes a startling, at times surreal, lyricism in this poetic narrative which fall as burning meteors, dark matters making light, to suddenly ascend into the love fall. Departing of parents within a short span fifteen months empties her into adult orphanhood; fallen, staggering along the convoluted memory lane of mirrors where dreamscapes merge in the back – forward – standstill of time. A scrambled time stream she chose to play in this play, "before I chose to become an egg." I wonder the confused question marks dancing in bone chamber minds reacting to her acknowledgement. That knowingly she picked her parents to set herself up in order to learn, or perhaps relearn, in this returned cycle. The lesson of unbounded heart love attachment to parents unexpectedly parting while knowing life is a death sentence."

> -Karl Kempton, *Sandskrit of Oceano Dunes;* Australia, 2021; *Selected Lexical & Visual Mathematical Poems 1976 - 2022*, 2022; *Portraiture: Oceano Dunes to Tide Line*, Australia, 2023; and chapbook, *Moon Shadows*, India, 2024.

"These are poems of vision. A view from above, watching, and noting. A view that will often come crashing down and mire itself in the earth, dirt, in bodies and plants. There is movement in the poems. From voice, to image, to the very shape of these poems there is breathlessness for the reader, a sense of falling and crashing from the words on the page. And a sense of rising back up. Falling down and falling up. And there is a beauty to the shape of these poems that leads us in this movement. Form here is stretched, pushed on, yet familiar and striking. This is a part of that movement, a part of the falling. These poems are breathtaking and beautiful, intimate and powerful, filled with images that rise and fall."

> -James Tyner. Author of *The Ghetto Exorcist,* First Poet Laureate of Fresno, California, and Librarian.

"The poems in this collection read like an instruction manual for living in the in-between, for living with loss and grief. There is an unblinking intelligence moving through these poems, reminiscent of Jorie Graham, but it is more than intelligence, as the speaker asks us to let go of the guardrails of reason, of the safety of the everydayness, to dive without knowing how it will turn out for us. It is a clear, steady beam of light we find in these pages, one guides us straight down into the center of the ache because ultimately, "Love is as strong as any death." These poems ask us to find our courage, ditch the "mind chatter," and surrender to "the raw center" of it all."

-Michelle Patton, Poet and Fresno City College English Professor.

"Parachuting, drifting, ascending, or plummeting in the realm of *Falling* paves way of exploration to excavate emotions shown through intimate testimonies in the space of a page, that even such emotions take within the self. Complete vulnerability, with its unwavering weight on both sides of a coin, are faced with a courageous approach on an earthly and etherical retrospect. It grapples the innermost self and identity to bubbling questions of primordial existence, the uncontrolled circumstances we find ourselves when earthbound, and the ebb and flows of love. Pilar's threading of words in conjunction to her unthreading of memories lend a cosmos-sized space for contemplation. She is an earth-diver, sharing her discoveries, explorations and happenstances of the heart with us. *Falling* is a mindful and emotional rendition of what it means to fall in, out, through...everywhere."

-Nia Onit, Poet, Visual Artist, and Student of Consciousness and Human Potential.

Falling

Poems by Pilar Graham

Stubborn Mule Press

Devil's Elbow, MO

Copyright © Pilar Graham, 2025

First Edition 1 3 5 7 9 10 8 6 4 2

ISBN: 978-1-958182-87-1

LCCN: 2024952562

Cover and title page artwork: by US Geological Society – US Department of the Interior. Earth as Art 6. "Irriated." Source Landsat 6. February 6, 2019. Public Domain.

All rights reserved. No part of this publication may be reproduced or transmitted in any form or by any means, electronic or mechanical, including photocopying, recording or by info retrieval system, without prior written permission from the author.

Stubborn Mule Press is a subsidiary of Spartan Press. You may visit us at spartanpresskc.com.

Acknowledgments

Previous poetry books by Pilar Graham:

Currents. Tourane Poetry Press. 2022.

Where some of these poems originally appeared:

"Lord's and Lord," "On the Third Day," and "Poem About a Small Bird Trapped Beneath A Caged Water Grate." *Voices Anthology.* Cold River Press. August 2023.

TABLE OF CONTENTS

III.

Special Thanks & Acknowledgments

To my mother's dear sister, and my aunt, Gloria Masyga, thank
you for helping me find my laugh again, after years of compounded
loss and unremitting grief. I hold an unfeigned appreciation since
throughout the duration of writing this book, you have elicited me
to be a self-advocate—using my voice, again. Thank you for holding
my place, and subduing my homesickness, while being my eyes,
amongst the family landscape of Minnesota. My poems hold
an evergreen-desire, a loving affinity, to be near Sugar Loaf, the
woods, and to feel the breeze of the Mississippi River.

Additional gratitude to Keith Ford, who continues to receive my
poetry for not only edits, but the in-depth, creative, and strategic
discussions of what the poem is working to say. I am blessed by
your brotherly solidarity, and your natural ability to understand me
as a person. I am beautifully reminded how it's not necessary to
explain myself, as I often feel I must, in greatly being misunderstood
as a poet, a woman, and a teacher. Your ability to find resolution,
order, and perspective—regardless in my creative or professional
pursuits—is consistently delivered from a place of creativity,
generosity, and peace.

For the brilliant-mystic poets, and my philosophical mentors,
Karl Kempton and Dave Boles. It took little time for both of
you to fully understand the art of falling—since you're both
already awake. Your involvement and professional guidance
during final development of the book have been illuminating.
You each have changed my life, and the extramundane revelations
continue. I am grateful for our sacred conversations, reflective
of a primordial-type language, and the value and appreciation
around actually reading and doing the research, which is critical
while residing at the base camp of the earthly consciousness.
A special tribute to your dear friend, the late D. R. Wagner. While

my encounter on earth with D.R. was brief, I owe him all my gratitude, in this divine timing, for his guidance in the *Falling* manuscript toward its rightful publishing path.

Special acknowledgments to Nia Onit. Your feedback and editorial comments on the manuscript have been instrumental. Your gracious contributions have not gone unnoted. Thank you to my Fresno City College colleague and poet, Michelle Patton who, without hesitation, stepped in to provide editorial feedback on the manuscript prior to publication. Our poetic friendship has always been free of disclaimers or complications. Heartfelt gratitude to James Tyner. Your invitations to read poetry and teach creative writing at the Clovis Community Library in 2009 initially carved out, not only the path of where I was about to travel, but established the groundwork in our friendship, with a poetic alliance that still continues to bear fruit. Special recognition to Vuong Vu, colleague, friend and founder of Tourane Poetry Press. You are brilliantly gifted in the discourse of critical analysis of poetry. Fused with your publishing talents, your articulate pursuit and poetic appreciation, as revealed in your dialogical and written responses, continually astounds me. Thank you, Jennifer Leahy, for reviewing a portion of the manuscript before going to print. A deep-heart acknowledgment to Carol Anderson for welcoming me into the Tribe.

An enormous recognition to my recently-discovered editor, Dolores, who is too humble to provide her full name. Thank you.

Heartfelt acknowledgements to both Maxine Hong Kingston and C. Lok Chua for your earlier support, including your writing endorsements for the printing and release of my previous poetry book, *Currents*. Your kindness and contributions have made a significant impact along the way. Unequivocally, your creative and scholarly publications continue to inspire, intellectually challenge, and embolden my creative energy. You are my scholars.

To my friend and academic colleague, Stephanie Spoto, who
showed me the way of the Carmel River, reminding me not
to take life so seriously, while your love and poetic-hospitality
continually ground me to the Monterey Bay area. More praise to
my CSU Monterey Bay students, who listened to several
of the poems—in all of their draft stages, while I attempted
to cognitively sort out what the poems wanted me to say.
This includes Tiva Rocco. The trust and transparency in our
friendship still continues to teach me how to be a better person.
Praise for Patience Ronyak-King, not just for your contagious
laughter in life, but the intellectual brilliance and contributions
you bring to any ethics and literature class. Thank you for being
one of my strongest supporters—especially during the mixed
intensities of being a poet, since it is seemingly unnatural to
separate me from my creative projects and pursuits.

Special thanks to Linda Schaedle who, on several occasions
throughout the course of this book, helped me find the words
in order "to get back up." You stood by me, and reminded me
of my resilience while I was falling, again and again, sometimes
literally against the earth. The extension of your empathy and
kindness, combined with your continual outreach, accessibility,
and reliability provided the trust I needed to return to an upright
position and keep moving forward. I will always carry your
kindness in my heart.

Additional gratitude to Carel Adler-Robin, Michael Robin, and
Daisy for checking in on me after the recent loss of my father.
I hold a deep appreciation while we spoke during my weekly, six-
hour commutes from mountains to ocean. Thank you for being
receptive in hearing the drafts of the poems and allowing me to
witness, through poetic sound, where and how to move to the
next version of the poem.

Deep appreciation for the Ordway family for reserving a place for me in your home and at your dining room table. Gratitude for Cat Hoffman in your assistance during my mountain absence. Your support grants me the ability to work in areas where I am called to serve. Special acknowledgements to Dana Crowley, who has known me since the sixth grade. Our history includes decades of California memories. I am grateful we live in the same mountain community and still have one another. Special acknowledgments to Audra Signes for your friendship and support with my poetry. Special gratitude to Victoria Terzian, for watching me fall in the early stages of this manuscript, while reminding me the book has its own "divine and beautiful pacing... reminiscent of a dance." Thank you, Victoria, for keeping alive the spirit of my mother, Cherie Greene, through your memories in your friendship with her. This has been an atypical gift, since her departure, and it does not go unnoticed. Hats off to my friend and stylist, Brittny Wattenburg, who reminds me that real beauty lives centered and deep in the spirit; yet, I am grateful for the chair, mirror, laughter, and love. Additional gratitude to Antonio Lopez, my friend and other stylist. Thank you for visually putting me together. Your honesty, kindness, and sense of humor always have a way to readjust any misalignments, given I am physically called to be in more than one place at a time in California.

To my Minnesota Paulsen family: Kirstin, Dave, Cassie, Ally, Charlie, and Autumn. A special and direct acknowledgement to my first earth-friend, Kirstin, who has consistently and unconditionally loved me—always leaving me with the impression that it's an easy task when I am aware of the complexities. Kirstin, thank you for reminding me of my home in Minnesota. I am to the right of you in the Jeep Wrangler. You can find me at Lake Louise in Le Roy, Minnesota, wrapped by the ancestral-spirit of my grandmother, Emily "Em" Hittner. Together, we are always exploring Sugar Loaf, walking on a green pasture and forever making our way to the water's edge. I love you.

Infinite love and high-dimensional gratitude to my friend, sister, and medium, Sherry Anderson. Your divine influence as my spiritual sister is always recognized and valued, whether spoken or telepathic. Your crystalized guidance, especially around the matters of love, have been instrumental—especially after having recently fallen for the first time.

A continual tribute to the messages and signs, including when I anthropomorphize objects discovered in the directional inspirations in the natural world most notably the ones that spoke to me throughout the course of writing this book. An hour doesn't pass when I don't think of my parents and how their worldly wisdom and generosity toward me was what initially introduced me to raw beauty. While writing this book, some of the confirmations from the natural world included: butterflies; hummingbirds; crows; the trees of southern Yosemite; the history and language found along bark; dating tree rings on tree stumps; the songs sung in the horizon of Heaven; cosmic strips of stars pressed into night; the planet Mars; unknown names, and the small species of messenger birds; the mountain ridge "Dragon Mountain"; fog; rain, thunder and lightning; pink amethyst geodes, rocks and crystals, named or otherwise; the shifting wind currents; the sun and the low-hanging moon; flowers and foliage; the Mississippi River; the arrival of darkness with its assurance for the arrival of Light; each entrance and departure of the four seasons; the molting and blooming of the earthly bodies; blackberries; the dropping of acorns; earth-scars; and the veil of hope that arrives with dusk—where I can read the love-messages—found only on the face of clouds.

Foreword

In the age of thirty-second sound bite messages, Pilar Graham's book, *Falling,* stands out from the current poetic trend of publishing poems that are easily decipherable; no need to spend an immense amount of time reflecting on the poem in front of you. Quickly scan the page, jump to the last line, and you are done. This is the blueprint for a modern book of poetry.

Falling, however, does not fit this mold. Blueprints were not considered. Alone. Unique. At times perhaps even harsh in its open truthfulness, *Falling* is a refreshing look into the heart of a poet's soul. You cannot quickly scan the pages and jump to the last line, comforting yourself with the inane notion that you understand what the poet has written. Far from it. These poems, these words, need time to decipher the intents of the poem and the poet. Plural, not singular, for there are many intents to unravel.

The first indication there is more here than meets the casual first glance of a poetry book is the eloquent introduction Pilar has given to help navigate the tome. Simple enough. Fairly straight forward even.

The poems that follow begin to shed light on the powerful message Pilar has laid out. This is not your normal "feel good" book of poetry. It is far more than that. Wrapping your head around these poems takes time, but the reader does begin to understand.

But then an odd occurrence takes place while reading on. A glimmer of intransigence is observed. What the reader thought they might have understood is quickly stripped away.

A reevaluation of lifelong indoctrination is sorely needed to continue. Where is the thirty-second sound bite both academia and society have indoctrinated in us? Where is the safety in poetry to which we have all become accustomed to? It is nowhere to be found. Yet, poems such as "Descent," "Planet of War," and "Released," give the reader enough pause to consider that perhaps a closer reading of the first two sections might be in order after all.

What the reader thought was true has now been shattered and reassembled before the book has even ended. This has enabled not only confusion, but illumination. There is a clarity to be found within these pages that is obscured by the gray tediousness of life. We are learning and falling simultaneously.

The last poem, "Dream of Falling to Rise To," nicely concludes the journey, and what a journey it has been. Pilar Graham has written not just a book of poetry, but a road map to consciousness. Of a life lived with love, infinite love, beginning while still in the womb, and carrying forth through life, *Falling* is indeed a complete weaving of infinite love. There are no sound bites here. No gimmickry. Only the sublime renditions of life and love, both within and without.

We should all be so fortunate to "fall" with the grace, beauty, and elegance that Pilar has illuminated within this tome.

Dave Boles
Publisher,
Cold River Press

For Rick

Falling

I.

2020 - 2022

To reach the center of grief, use thyme—
burned once in temples for courage.
Now move: opposite in direction, and
into the unfamiliar. This is you now.
Remove the teardrops for leaves—
use only your fingers. Refrain from
any intellect on how to survive and
allow yourself to slide down the center;
feel life press against the evergreen and

slip away from the earth. Isolation enters
home. More directions: A business card
of my attorney is taped to the face of a fridge
("In case you find me dead"). Call her first
and line things up—I may not come back.
Having entered the raw center of this place,
my mother, flown from her body, or
my father, mid-March—my last eye-to-eye.

Living Trust

Light yourself on fire
in the kitchen   but only
if you mean it
otherwise
learn to point the flame
towards the tealight
where you signal solace.

Face forward   repeat
the prayers.
Life will find a way
to grow
even while it builds a nest
on the sun's back
on the neck of madness
and lights shout   *turn it off.*

I work
to decipher the narratives
in my hand
a gallery   black and white photos
1944
before my father begins
the family root
before the second coming
of my quiet Absence
before I chose to be an egg.

You've departed now
you see all.
Candle me
with flame
as you did when you were fifteen years old
tucked away   in the back room of the *A&P*
a local market   in our   old world
                    in our   Michigan
egg after egg
when you knew how to separate
the ones in front of you
knew how to separate
the bad   from the good.

            You're dying
you say: *remain here*
amongst the life
and with the rest
on earth
            even with those
who have failed living
with trust
choosing their cosmic cautions
for the afterlife.

Double Membrane

Rescue us
from this sidewalk
of the unattainable.
Your voice takes
root, swims as if
fashioned in cells.
Mitochondria, you say
as he slips under
another mirage
bent by time
only to obscure the idea
of embrace

a type of human
connection
when lovers
live in remote.

February at the Monterey Poetry Group

untucking ourselves
from pleats   now fanned
inside a candlelit house

you can pass us
on the streets without knowing
the dialogue
or the calm urgencies   rising
like sky-witches
who point to a center-verse
above the rows of roofs
as they watch with one eye
as they fly in all Four Directions
past the exposed ribs
our ribs
the roof ribs
made from the same
vaulted & seasoned wood

we work
to listen to ourselves   speak
from all the beings
unseen
or too seen   too much
and burn ourselves
like incense
no longer clay
displaced pots
trying to find placement

after being stored
too far back
          inside journals
          using our only   voice
          as our makeshift chairs

Leaving

one could die in this cliché
hope only for life
after death
swirl yourself up
inside the belly
of self- crippling
comma- shaped state
tails and tales turn
its back to the west
motion brings life
to any aliens transports
for only those who work
to trace the steps
forgotten in the blinds
within any home-space
feel your way out from
this comma dead-space
always incomplete
sickness in reason
or what is grossly misplaced
enter storage leave your body
out out out stack your history
in a box in summertime
build towers paper windows
hallways and doors
that lead to the Mississippi
feel her watery back
a silted soul calling out scents
of sun splitting by thousands

a memory   inside childhood
nose to tail   until you return
no dream   poem or song-
death   is not final
the empyreal   visible now

mother, Other: Palimpsest

all these clocks   tick acid
at once   but each off
by a second   they will never
be set at the same
time   like we all thought   or how
or who   would go first   or how
i would be the last   left to listen
to time with all of your clocks
        then   there is my time
my hands are somewhere
in this house of your death
        the face of
your bedroom clock
watches over me   even
the weight on my back
        for three years   i have swapped out
your absence with *another*
battery   for all the clocks
one lives in another
like Other lives in mOther
      you are still somewhere here
between the leaves of the palm
in your bedroom   there by the window
& jewelry squirreled in corners
thetoplefthandside
of your black lacquered dresser drawer

II.

On the Third Day: Flower Series

Remember to still hold us with your fiery hands.
Here, walls press out; you can find us upright now
like mortal cups—veins deepened with inky Sun-desire.

Hair-like breath lives in this earthly garden, where
pulses twist together, working by day to grow
before the Dark, sexed only by the sounds of spring.

Gendered colonies are constantly pivoting.
Cosmic orange hues speak in tongues amongst their kin,
their bodies bloom beneath botanical bed sheets;

the Earth now decides what to bless and who will be
the last to survive. After the rains, we center our bodies,
lean in closer—a post-newborn separation—yielding from

one another; an eternal wilt after the absence of any Sun.

Poem About a Small Bird Trapped Beneath
a Caged Water Grate

For Rick

It was either male

or female   a neologism

of flight reduced

three inches   from a riddle

beneath a rusted-wired sky

from all the human designs

to keep waste and debris out.

The bird is reduced to vision

and peers through a honeycomb of

weathered grooves   for windows

and waits   on the other side

      where   life

      and   thought

      equals   freedom

      and   reduction

      lives   daunting

      a   space

      now   grounded.

Surrender is never the same

even when   free from entanglement

songs are rarely heard   using one's own breath.

Flight risks   fatality

only when windborne

and left to scratch   for treasures

within fallen ignorance

along the surface of the earth.

Lord's and Lord

We're near the gallows

        and not supposed to

        say anything.   Don't say

        The Word   too loud

        or how it may feel

        as it lands   face down

        avoidance is heaviest

        in its betrayal

        after the weight

        breaks the necks

        of the highest dahlias heads.

The King Tide is here   at the lip

        of the land   spilling petals

        from its mouth   mortality frays

        and instability begins

        to split

        its own mouth   wide open

        from the gnashing of its own teeth.

Look the other way

        without rolling

        your eyes   a nonverbal dissent

        like aged   particles

        as if   we were subjects

        living safe inside

the underwater sea   but only

serfs tucked beneath

the clean cuffs   of a lord's pant.

These directions lead me

nowhere home   instead

it's a trapping   like an itch

deep below the river's skin

until the currents which

begin   to shape us

tell us

what we were born to hear.

This is not a grave

but the turning of the middle

ages of the light

towards the marketplace—

stands of life

nesting in crystal wicker

beneath the snaps and the claps

from rows of kingdom-home flags.

I see you   again   all of you

before me   within me.

We are no longer fractured

but movements within light

embracing   the afterlife

part of the cosmos

and now able to be

in more

than only one place.

God save the... king?

Don't look back

at the all perversion   now

there's no need   to translate

we've all reached the same place.

The animals are having a barn dance.[1]

---

[1] Tom T. Hall. *Songs of Fox Hall.*

Sky-Stone

This is our atmosphere:
lusty inversions found
in earth-bound bodies;

watch us fold into night,
forming like naturals using
hip and breath. It's time

to wake, dear— *awake*—
before the flight, wilding our
nature with stratospheric souls.

Dating Tree Rings

I can't remember   the year
when I could   not   wait
so I ate   for love

I moved   under the California bark
as a wood boring beetle
marking the trails only to

count the growth
the rings   of the tree
of you   and   me

where two souls oscillate & split
stories from unspoken pasts   finally
hollow me   out

so we can   find life
fashion me   with your hands
cut me   to the ground

a wellspring of joyous sound   found
you will find me here   post-scored
now   love-sanded smooth

together   from all the years past
homesick   treesick   lovesick
each ring a cycle   from where

this tree   from where we stand

in this moment

feel the goodness of the grain

my body now   vulnerable   at best.

Blade

I.
Locusts are in the garden
of my senses
around the olive tree

Lumber arrives
as a gift of split trees
under the passing
of black clouds where lightning
the mechanic says
is always part of thunder
and says to me
I was taller when I dropped
my truck off nine hours ago
yet my heels-to-sandals
have not changed my height
when I watch myself grow taller
in front of you
or how I hold
my hand and create a shield
for my forehead
with all there is
with all the raindrops stealing
my attention
within this indescribable
moment
wet with a high-musk scent

II.

Locust looks a bit like *lo*-ve

But this one is no longer solitary

and against the nature of their history

or the order of things

even in this migration where

bugged-eyed omens swarm

in their seasonal signs

in current time

yet could it be possible

the wrath of God

from all ten plagues

is finally beginning to lift

III.

I collapse

the stacked boxes

moving around the one-dimensional

darkness

and the looming contents:

California   dry of wild honey

where here

not even the locusts can claim a King

I reach back to the homeland

along the Mississippi River

where annual blue grass

lives amongst white cedars

and osprey

who fly above fox snakes and

rule over the yellow bass becoming

splinters of absconded light beneath

the surface of river-generations

where Catholic churches

join together like milkweed

and braid themselves

tightly inside

the safety of your smile

or the wind

where destination fails

to be translated

while you dance around the sword

either at the pommel

or the point

and perhaps lost

to the sound

since any courage is likely to look

different to each man

Sky-Locked

We stand together and I am secure
in your ability to steer;
it's the way you usher me away
from this spectrum...
a semi-grounded haze,
a hardpan for a horizon.
Be the first to remove me
from this rust-colored gaze.

You tell me to *look* at the sky, and I say:
When did we stop looking up?
When did we lose our way?
How did we become so calibrated
and masterful, learning to step
over the lofty formations
just above our crowns?

In the fraction/freeform,
in the shape of self-detachment,
we *could* join together and become weightless... skyward,
as if earthy shapeshifters
in a spectacle of skyscraping love.

Right now,
the only confirmation are the cumulus clouds.
And yet, I am left not entirely sure of this experience:
could it have been something
formed by my own demise?

Reunion with the Earth's Distance

Two miles—now, over two hundred—
by way of water and mountains.

I speak, but it's unknown if you
can hear me through this stretch

where my insides travail
like the California Sister you've

catalogued in the world
with butterfly flight,

and so, I imagine your saying hello
again, this time to a bird passing by

outside my garden home, where
you once told me, wearing blue

eyes, that I was blessed, yet I know
love is as strong as any death. [2]

[2] Reference: Song of Solomon. 8:6.

Serenity Prayer: Third Summer Without You

With the heaviness

of the afternoon

inside

the chest cavity

I hear my mother

clear her throat—

She's about to say

something

anything

reminding me

the best way to surrender

through the kitchen window

amongst the mad barks

of the summer blue jays

Before You Leave

In response to: Ecclesiastes 3:19

Remember to take the useless rifle
and break it against the tree. Even in solitude

you can follow your way back to your camp;
watch out for the wolfish and what the snares found...

left behind by the wilderness beasts. Now you are
the scouting party. In order to survive, you will learn

to put the bridle reins in your teeth (if you have to).
You hear along the way, distant family members

saying, you are the archivist of the family. Days later, you read:
"...the fate of beasts is the same, as one dies so dies another."

Waiting at the Gate

From this place
new horizons   are taking shape
in the mind   of her mind

You might be surprised   how far
    she has come along this mountain trail.

Love makes itself known   shadow dances
    in hoof beats
across the newly-opened sky   as birds sing
    at the back door
of your new house
of beginnings   and finally   from dying oneself
.

Come on by
the breeze is really moving
through her castle-like waves of hair
as if life itself   is twisting on its ends
as if   twirling peace and war   together
as if   it has waited all day through tremor
to finally see   you

It's not just in the way   you sit next to her
on the steps   or how
lip-words are secondary in nature
or how   in the distance
as if closed in   and captured
and once   again
or for   the first time

the way love moves its hips in front of you
or how
it has decided to move   at its cobblestone click-clack
using the chords
cutting her deep
to the quick
or how   everything will finally lift
like blood-soaked gardenias
as if
old grief drying and flaking
right from your blade
right before your eyes
where everything, again,   has finally lifted
from the low-hanging Sierra clouds
of what seems   like any other Saturday
but yet
past   the normal beat of life

she's onto something
something outside herself
and falling to the wayside   from your sword
as it cuts   again   and quick to the edge
of the green
and into the terrace
of her wild senses   yet
there's a moment
where redemption finds a way to rise
by the *soundoftone* of your voice   or how
it carries   eye-to-eye
and shields   her
from what she cannot begin to see,
even denial is captured
soft

like your leathery hands
slicing away   at edge of reason   and yet
she remains convinced
this is all part
of the ethical order
or accord

She knows
she is not of this world;

consecrate the keyboard.

It will be okay…
that is what *he* would say…
should say…

I say, keep listening to *Requiem*
          it will all make sense
you need to lose your mind first
trust   first
the Epilogue of the Divine
hang your head
down
let your hair
gravitate
like a mare whose finally found
in the twilight
alone
before the castle gates close
regardless of the wars
that have passed
or those yet to come

Falling

Catch me
by the tree stump
with my hand   outstretched   now
against the five rings of growth
my fingers   fanned
and flattened
against only my visible   senses
if time   is included
and only   in remnants
of dust
the powdery memory
of mulch
or how longing   can scatter
and become the focus
when facing the ground
yet   I don't think about
the three types of tears
since the eternal will
wipe them all away
or at least   may grow anemones
and cover the surface of isolation
when it attempts to carve itself
down to a number
after it whittles away
using cuts without any measure
and after   apart from *this* reality
and later   the derealization will settle in

from the crosscut of this couch

and the sightlines   from the window

begin to curve

towards the forestry of green hips

a wilderness   a body   my body

and how   even the earth

is always bending   against its own gravity

and constantly falling

or how   even a fixed horizon

suspends the heaviest of weight

becoming a winded denial

or how   I might represent to you

as if

I would be different

instead

merely a variation of another sin

a temptation

that finds life   across the yellow rails

and has ability to move   back

and forth

and makes up for itself

with the sacred   offerings

behind the Virgin's back

as you edge walk

after having already mastered

that mendacious shapeshifting

from the center   of your bona fide heart

against the terrain of risk

while envy-milling the arrival

of your grained-restraint

as I fall back against the earth
to count the circles
of spalted wood at the rise of today's dawn
now   nothing is one dimensional
my body is falling   for the first time
against the skin of the drum

Rock

Let's agree on one thing:
to meet on Holy Ground
since we have much to do
in this realm, here and now,
where trust cannot clamor
or follow the mind chatter
which lays their generational
traps on green-mossed earth,
as it was for our forefathers,
or how, between two brothers,
it began with the clenching
of rock temples and only to
crush Mercy, using skull to skull.

Roman Soldiers

heavy pens lean
on the station
of the cross   while iron works against
the Body
but   remember this
we are   in the echo chamber
and inside the tomb
or how it works
with wood   all laced with slants
against the grain of blood-leather
where we know   nothing
about the nail bags
or the precedent
of the weight   or the gravity of wearing
the irregularities   or the commonalities
found in the single voice
of our written history
when they asked   to put the feet *together*
when all that was left   were only three nails.

Someone Used a Yellow Bandana as a Shawl
on the Virgin Mary

My bass range says,
don't let me slip away,
while low notes fashion me
as I long for a yellow bandana
to be placed around me—
like the one we witnessed in the Garden
where random mercy worked
to unfreeze the Virgin Mary—
a solitary statue amongst trees
under moon and leaves,
before the night cleanses itself,
before it becomes unseen
amongst an era
of earth-bound figures;
my repetitions keep me warm.

And later, I hear *your* voice,
praying to another,
another version of longing,
becoming an audible ballad
against the contour of my upright ear.
It's a series of melodies
solely dependent on one another,
a poetic version of your language
presenting an ensemble,
an unveiling of a nomadic harmony,

until we begin to orbit
along the yellow threads
stitched by the holiest of stars.

III.

Descent

There's no way to pace yourself, not even the
　　blackberry on the tongue
can be rushed. Take your time, allow the body to freefall

against the sky-currents and allow the filter to look for
　　the pout of clichés.
This is not a drill. This is not for everyone, especially
　　not onlookers from the hill.

You're retiring, but the ocean will remain, even in your
　　absence. Letting go
is not to forget—it's nothing more but fogged-in wind. Trust

how you will land—it will be the antidote for content
　　without messing with the voice—
since pacing is never reliable, and the shape of any
　　mood starts out in a flat tone.

Take your body, trace outside the lines and move with
　　the curve of worldly
dimensions of evolution. There is no help, but to let it
　　all drain out from what lives

inside the walls of organization, rearrangement, or
　　derangement. Rely on your voice;
there's nowhere else to look. Snap the sheet and hold it
　　against the window.

Accept you'll fall in love—for the first time—while you
    write the *Falling* manual,
again and again, knowing we are only one part moving
    around the larger living myth.

Planet of War

A prompt for freestyle begins,
all within its divine order
to save you
from the euphoria
that has taken hold of your body,
your mind,
and how it now twists
in tangents of conflict,
while still being cataloged
as a correspondence,
becoming the grounds
for a new argument.

The fall from grace prepares... let it
move from the inside out
(since it's already in motion)
where the heart debates
if it should close
as if
your voice becomes
trapped—
there are no more words
or songs
left to save you
from the shadows
that we blame on the full moon,
or how Aries is on fire
this day, month, year,
ruled by Mars.

Only an eclipse is prone
to hide
using its shadow.
Just let it be what it is for now:
a change in seasons,
as the acorns
fall louder than years before.

Listening to "Songbird"

Fleetwood Mac. Released February 1977.

Before the separation,
you sung the lyrics to me
"I love you"
the only way
I know how, even though
in your renditions,
I never looked for rhyme, only a confirmation of
  repetitions.

This is the story of a song and how
it became part of printed
history,
the day it became adhered
firmly living on my refrigerator,
a memento
from another recording
of a sort
which had been years
with a flip-turn in selflessness,
sound-sincerity,
as I witnessed the first page
of my journal,
after all these years,
slipping out, and releasing itself
from me, splitting away
from hand-stitched seams…

False-Positive

It *could* have been a first kiss,
but instead, I bought the book in blue
for you, and began to plummet in my fire sign,
          waiting and writing,
          writing and waiting
for the trees to clap,
a heavenly reverence of wisdom and beauty
at winter's start and into the wilderness-
          warmth that could melt wax
at the root chakra. It's about you
and how your eyes
pass for gems,
          watching me
          watch them
glistening along unforeseen facets,
a spectral-invite to this place of
dreamlike dimensions,
          but now…it is cerebral,
freshly-presented paradoxes
and parables, as to whether or not
our lips will ever-join
          ever-beneath
the October Sky
and finally, rain washed us straight
with blood rubies—everywhere.
          Can we skip to the chorus line?

Released

Today, this is what it feels like to fall head first
from the center and trace the lover's latitude—

steps that move back and forth across dubious
terrain, imaginary lines across the Body's border—

you will survey new territory; another loss in life,
denoting the survivors from the inept casualities of summer

forcing our wide-open mouths to form new languages
from the freefalling; a collapse from sky to earth offers

nothing real to touch. Crudeness scars the path.
Convince yourself: *close your heart*, it's the only way

to avoid, or pivot, around this place of reeling distinction.
And so, I keep my eyes on the ridgeline in the distance,

since the highest points of my sentience still remain,
as the edge of reason verifies: here, nothing is safe again.

krip-toh-mnee-zhuh

As memory tries to serve, it was a season of senses, after we innately entered the course of things; even the phenomenal has an ability to allude to earth-bound scars. We drifted above the ponderosa pines—branches away, from the aerial of our indifference, while the illusive worked to cascade, slow and silent like stalactites, unaware of the approach of surface tension. How easily we confuse into self-erasure, where we work to readjust our aureoles. From this place, we suspend in the parallel universe, leaving leftovers of Phantom-love-orbital-exhaust. From this distance, we retell the stories, a recollection gathered and measured, using our height above the ground. It is possible you have mistaken me for another memory? As if I had been your skyward song, an eidetic embrace, a flashback of some sort, only to serve, as if a product of your memory.

Freefall

There is a difference
> between transcending and descending,
> since with each,
> the position cannot be abandoned;
> any vessel without an anchor
> is apt to be ill-savored by sin.

This isn't about the sake of saving yourself
> with works from the earth;
> intent only cleanses one so far.

A decline won't always show you
> what's coming—
> falling can console,
> even trick,
> using its arms as
> in the unforeseen rapture;
> it's always the first sign,
> illusions preclude
> the insincerity of in-love.

Shadows will find their own homes
> amongst the highest of skies.
> Do not cast your sights on the horizon;
> it was your vulnerability
> that left you bare, left you to witness.

Arrivals will find new introductions,
       but your soul will remain;
       it's okay to be *damaged*.
       Inside this place,
       we only look for love.
       Go ahead and fall,
       fall into this fazed place,
       and find solace in the holes
       until you edge yourself out from injustice.

This is how we measure
       your being
       from what seems
       like the ground, when
       actually, it's the highest form
       of your formidable truth.

Post-Downslope: Measures of Self Arrestment

I.

It was the fourth, and natural reason, of my role, my
    superimposed anima.
When I look back at the body of the same mountainside, it's
    as if I believed
retrospection *could* move clockwise, recite the angle of
    inclination, strangely
coupled with seasonal irrelevance and logic, or how, the lack
    of ability

did not deter our reasoning for flight, or how I failed to see
    the naked weight
of the steadfast of gravity, or to let it run its course.
    Instead, we lost our breath,

the sky had become fear-swiped and fallen off its axis.
    No Instructions provided,
except: "Coordinates are subject to disconnect, an autumn
    love-haze may blind."

II.

It was no more than entangled moments, or the results of
    being branched
apart, the motion of being forced downward, leaving spirals
    to snip, for us
to slip, until we allowed ourselves to fall into the quiet, self-
    made disclosures,
while our bodies heard the release of our loudest scream;
    we work to forget

from the day, as for the memory of the mountain... we fell
     mute and positioned
toward what separates us from day and night, the sublime,
     becoming an ethereal
sweetness in surrender—its body, a downward loss towards
     confusion, a mere
dilemma, a mid-air collision, the result of division, splitting
     us—two miles apart.

III.
Only during midair can the answers take us back to how it
     might have been
if we had simply jumped first, or learned to love out-of-
     balance even in our ex-
earthly air positions; without trying, it might have been
     possible to land—feet first.
In self-arrestment, there's nothing to brace; impacts will
     result in sweeter fruit.

Reason cannot live inside post-intellect, nor find a way to
     the piedmont. There are
no song-prayers to help either of us levitate so instead,
     I say: *go ahead and land on me.*
I await your arrival in my constant collapse. Lift your eyes
     from the monkey flower.
You are not alone. When the mountain crumbles, there will
     be nowhere left to run.

The Order of Fog

1. This is an older, and low-living marsh narrative,

2. where I work to position myself to look up,

3. a resident from underneath the veneers of truth;

4. it's part of the process, they say, that nests in thickets,

5. or the way to survive the vapors—set yourself free.

6. But solace is slippery and subjective, especially for the unrooted,

7. or the wildly-untethered, where desires have to learn

8. to uncoil each morning, and to rinse the mud out clean,

9. from the blurred perspective, where silences can no longer

10. resist the blue of droplets, its feet now, dangling midair.

11. Above the treetops, while the rest of the natural habitat remains

12. love-bound, it continues to grow upward and together, even while

13. the melancholy of the forest sighs, continual echoes along the way...

14. ~~What are you saying to me?~~

15. There are no directional winds, or stars, visible from this view.

16. It's only at this particular hour, the snowy egret begins to separate

17. from her colony and starts to skim the surface of surrealistic chance,

18. displaying her skills, once away from all others, and using

19. its rope-like neck to take a final bow, into the fluid
reflections,

20. without having to position the body, so as to not ever
look back.

Full Moon Falling

The moon could not be any more full;
its heavy hip pivots away from earthshine,

its early-day entrance makes contact, wants me
to accept its cyclical mood—it will pass, too...

like summer, where the orbitual weight of truth
lives in each season, or how isolation can speak

in a series of arrivals and departures.
My body, phase-bound, will need to feel

through an unaccounted and untraversed space
of growth and decline—the universal travesties

that move against what we are, or simply doing
what we are being asked to do or not to do.

Take me away from sides of light and dark,
instead, to the fire, to the wild element,

to the roots at the center of your eyes, and where
the blushing landscape and sky can finally fuse.

Dream of Falling to Rise To

I. Dream of Falling

It's the trite-edged rim of fear, mixed & misguided
    misallocations—
simply the grounds for another evening's rise above
    falsehood, a sobering

type of rebalance, before I wake from my dreams, where
    two worlds
become breathless; their disarray a notable conflict. I
    think about you

yours--& the others, while they chalice the cup,
    interdimensional portals,
as if, one could slip away, even momentarily & back into a
    circular relapse,

& into the forbidden, where river-blood will always carry
    us back together
from the hidden spaces of history, where riddles &
    remissions rescind. My mouth

presses in, partly by age, partly by reason, and notes
    prescribed by rituals, as if holy
confirmations with communion work to comfort the
    mouth & mind, where knees

come together & kneel—another version of a self-
    vindication, or love, but no—
it will remember to leave lip-traces, since it was only a
    pretense of blood-stains.

II. Rise To

Dedicated to August 1969

It was our partial flat-bellied land,
historically hushed in nature, figure
heads have grown from the wild
rice—narrow and low-hanging
tornados can skim
channels into Leo-shaped crests
absent of a timeworn trace,
other than the silt that slips
from the river's mouth, cups
of water carried by ancestral ghosts,

the sandbank-weavers before us,
and before them, while knowing
the difference between the two—
as with any midwest afternoon,
in early spring, found in memory
of the neighborhood moments.
You will find ways to swim

from the two paleographic
landscapes, custom-made to stretch
their long backs along the wood rows,
weathered piers and back house decks.

This one is a sunbather: she is of the Mississippi,
this is mother, this is me.
Using a barely-formed hand,
I reach from inside you,
using only a tip of an arrowhead
for a heart. Expect the chips to fall
before it's formed, since I am about to bear
an earth name. Find ways to speak,
in the months to come, and press
against the three linings
of seasons, a stratum of tissue.

In decades of clan-gathering,
they will say, *this one is different... special.*
I already knew the poet's postpartum,
forceps that clasp, without using voice,
having felt the strange curl leaving
the entrance of warmth,
the kind found having lived inside her body,
and how the solar sun is always the first

to implant any introductions of life
to the other side on earth—just around the time
the third-eye of the family
began to open
for me—freedom is found in fluidity,
a cellulous lining of
silken flesh that swaddles me
with clarity, with distractions

of glitter from the eyes, tubed off
in a life-love, from one generation

to the next, archivist-to-archivist,
while blood-veined-trees spike,
as they, too, gravitate towards
an upward in the early moments
of my spilled and cloudy ink-spells
inside the slow of flow motion, often shared

by the membranes of this telepathic potion,
inside departures which hollow out, as with any new home.

Pilar Graham is the author of *Currents* (2022). Her poetry has appeared in *Cold River Press - Voices Anthology; Gasconade; Sundog; Haunted Waters Press; Indent Literary Journal; Finishing Line Press; Blackberry,* among others. Publications for her creative nonfiction essays include *Essay Daily; The Broiler: A Journal of New Literature; Poetry Midwest;* and *Pithead Chapel Press.* Graham has served as a literary editor and a judge for local and national writing competitions. Graham earned her MFA in Poetry from California State University, Fresno and teaches at California State University, Monterey Bay and part-time for Fresno City College. Graham is currently seeking publication for her third collection of poems, *Forever, Becomes,* in addition to a collection of creative nonfiction essays, *Burn Scars,* www.pilargraham.com

This project was made possible, in part, by generous support from the Osage Arts Community.

Osage Arts Community provides temporary time, space and support for the creation of new artistic works in a retreat format, serving creative people of all kinds — visual artists, composers, poets, fiction and nonfiction writers. Located on a 152-acre farm in an isolated rural mountainside setting in Central Missouri and bordered by ¾ of a mile of the Gasconade River, OAC provides residencies to those working alone, as well as welcoming collaborative teams, offering living space and workspace in a country environment to emerging and mid-career artists. For more information, visit us at www.osageac.org

Osage Arts Community

www.ingramcontent.com/pod-product-compliance
Lightning Source LLC
Chambersburg PA
CBHW030509130626
46549CB00007B/2915